Victorian Britain

Mary Speed

Linked to the Local Community in Victorian Times

Oxford University Press 1994

The publishers wish to thank the following
for permission to reproduce copyright material:

Front cover: reproduced by permission of The Victoria and
Albert Museum; p.1 The National Motor Museum, Beaulieu; p.5
Manchester Central Library; p.6 Tony Lakin; p.12 top Mary
Evans Picture Library, bottom The Hulton Deutsch Collection;
p.13 The Hulton Deutsch Collection; p.15 Mary Evans Picture
Library; p.16 Mary Evans Picture Library; p.17 Mary Evans
Picture Library; p.18 The Hulton Deutsch Collection; p.20
Manchester Central Library; p.21 Mary Evans Picture Library;
p.22 Tate Gallery, London; p.23 top Greater London Record
Office, Map & Print Collection, bottom The Hulton Deutsch
Collection; p.24 top The Hulton Deutsch Collection, bottom Tate
Gallery, London; p.26 Christie's London/Bridgeman Art Library;
P.28 top Alison Anholt White, centre National Trust
Photographic Library/Andreas von Einsiedel, bottom Royal
Doulton Ltd; p.29 Mansell Collection; p.30 top Mansell
Collection, bottom Fine Art Photographic Library Ltd; p.31 top
Guildhall Art Gallery, London/Bridgeman Art Library, bottom
Mansell Collection; p.32 top NRM/Science and Society Picture
Library, bottom Royal Holloway & Bedford New College/
Bridgeman Art Library; p.33 NRM/Science and Society Picture
Library; p.34 The Illustrated London News Picture Library; p.35
top John Brennan, Oxford, bottom Sutcliffe Gallery, Whitby; p.36
The Francis Frith Collection; p.37 top Mary Evans Picture
Library, centre left and right The National Motor Museum,
Beaulieu, bottom Trustees of the Imperial War Museum,
London; p.38 top Mary Evans/Bruce Castle Museum, bottom
Peter Speed; p.39 top The Hulton Deutsch Collection, centre The
National Motor Museum, Beaulieu, bottom Mansell Collection;
p.40 top Mansell Collection, bottom Fine Art Photographic
Library Ltd./Mr and Mrs R. Holmes; p.41 Beamish, The North
of England Open Air Museum; p.42 Peter Speed; p.43 top
Greater London Photograph Library, centre and bottom Peter
Speed; pp.44-5 Peter Speed; back cover Fine Art Photographic
Library Ltd.

Illustrations by: Robert Ayton, John Brennan, Richard Hook,
John James, Bernard Long, Chris Molan and Tony Morris.

Oxford University Press, Walton Street, Oxford OX2 6DP

Oxford   New York   Toronto
Delhi   Bombay   Calcutta   Madras   Karachi
Petaling Jaya   Singapore   Hong Kong   Tokyo
Nairobi   Dar es Salaam   Cape Town
Melbourne   Auckland   Madrid

and associated companies in
Berlin and Ibadan

Oxford is a trade mark of Oxford University Press

© Oxford University Press, 1994

ISBN 0 19 917226 9

Typeset and designed by Positif Press, Oxford
Printed in Hong Kong

To the reader

Queen Victoria came to the throne in 1837.
She died in 1901. The people of Britain who
were alive during her reign are known as the
'Victorians'.

This book is about the Victorians. Quite
soon you will meet two children. One is
Thomas Clarke, a factory boy from Leicester.
The other is Ann Ambler, a girl coal miner.
Both were real people. They lived in early
Victorian times. First of all, we shall see
what life was like for them and many other
folk. Later, we will go forward to 1901 and
look at some of the changes that had taken
place over the years.

Time line

1837	Victoria becomes Queen
1838	London to Birmingham Railway
1840	Victoria marries Prince Albert
1841	Great Western Railway
1842	Mines Act. Women and children forbidden to work underground
1847	Simpson discovers anaesthetics
1848	Cholera epidemic
1850	5000 miles of railway completed
1851	Great Exhibition
1854	Cholera epidemic
1856	Bessemer process for making steel
1859	Lenoir invents gas engine
1860	Pasteur discovers microbes
1861	Death of Prince Albert
1863	First London Underground Railway
1866	Siemens process for making steel
1867	Cholera epidemic
1870	Lord Lister uses antiseptics
1876	Compulsory education
1877	Victoria given title 'Empress of India'
1884	Daimler invents petrol engine
1885	Invention of 'safety bicycle'
1887	Victoria's Golden Jubilee
1888	Benz makes first motor cars. Dunlop invents pneumatic tyre
1890	French produce rayon
1891	First electric tram
1896	Speed limit raised from 3 to 14 mph
1897	Victoria's Diamond Jubilee
1898	First motor buses
1901	Death of Queen Victoria

Contents

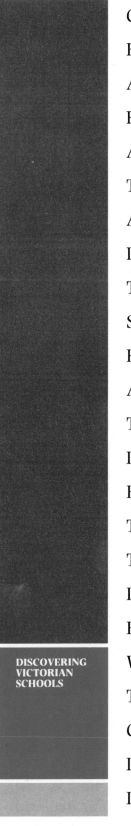

DISCOVERING VICTORIAN SCHOOLS

Cotton becomes king – the 1830s

Look closely at a piece of cotton cloth, such as a handkerchief. You will see threads crossing each other. The threads are made by twisting tiny fibres together. This is called **spinning**. The threads are then criss-crossed to make cloth. This is called **weaving**.

Look at Figure 1 below. When was cotton first used in Britain?

Even in the 1770s people in Britain were making very little cotton cloth. But it was very different in the 1830s. Every year they made enough to go round the Equator eleven times. This was an important change. Let's discover why it happened.

First of all, there had to be plenty of raw cotton. This is cotton when it is picked from the plant. It grows in fluffy balls. For a long time raw cotton came from Egypt. There was not much of it.

Look at Figure 2 below. What happened after 1780?

Fig 1 When different fibres were used.

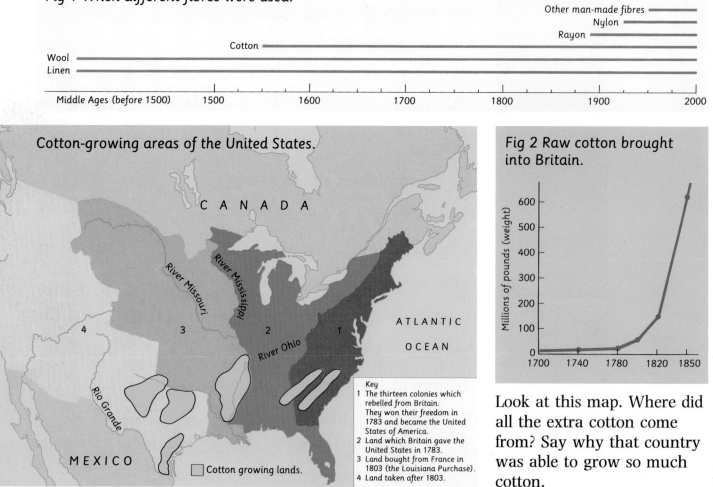

Cotton-growing areas of the United States.

Key
1 The thirteen colonies which rebelled from Britain. They won their freedom in 1783 and became the United States of America.
2 Land which Britain gave the United States in 1783.
3 Land bought from France in 1803 (the Louisiana Purchase).
4 Land taken after 1803.

☐ Cotton growing lands.

Fig 2 Raw cotton brought into Britain.

Look at this map. Where did all the extra cotton come from? Say why that country was able to grow so much cotton.

Something was also happening in Britain. They found new ways of spinning and weaving. At one time, spinning and weaving was done in the home. The mother and daughters did the spinning. They used spinning wheels.

Have you ever seen a spinning wheel? If so, where?

The father did the weaving. The photograph below shows him at work.

Why is his loom called a handloom?

After 1780 there was too much raw cotton for spinning wheels and handlooms. There had to be changes.

CLASS ACTIVITY
Look at the labels inside some of your garments. They will tell you what fibres are in the garments. Make a list of the fibres. Which are natural and which are synthetic? How long has each fibre been used in Britain? Is cotton still king?

Look at the picture of power looms below. Compare it with the photograph showing a handloom. What changes had taken place?

Look again at the power looms. Find the belts that drive the machines. Find the drums that drive the belts. They are turned by a huge steam engine. Why are the looms called power looms?

After the machines were invented, people could no longer work in their homes. They had to work in factories. Why was that?

Most of Britain's cotton factories were in and around Manchester and Glasgow. Find these places on a map.

Results of changes in the cotton industry

The changes in the cotton industry had many results. Here are just a few.

Look at this diagram. How did the change in price over the years help ordinary people, do you think?

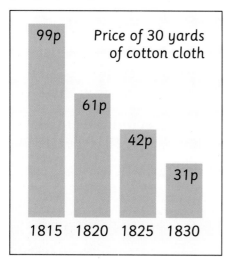

99p Price of 30 yards of cotton cloth

61p

42p

31p

1815 1820 1825 1830

Other people copied the cotton industry. Up till about 1840, all sorts of things had been made by hand, in the home. Among them were gloves, hats, buttons, nails, chains, locks. Now, more and more goods were made by machines, in factories.

The old machines were worked by hand. The new factory machines needed much more power. The first factories used water wheels like the one here. But what happened in dry weather, do you think?

Lady Isabella water wheel, Isle of Man. This was one of the biggest water wheels ever made. What is its diameter, roughly? (Use the people as 'rulers'.)

6

It was better to have steam engines. James Watt developed an engine in the 1770s. Later, Richard Trevithick and other inventors made much more powerful engines.

There were new factories to make machines and steam engines. We call this industry 'engineering'.

Soon, Britain was selling goods all over the world. To make sure it had customers, it built up a huge empire. The people in the empire had to buy British goods.

What did they send Britain, in return?

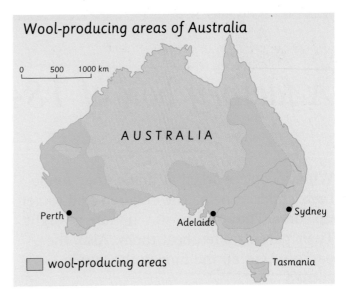

Wool-producing areas of Australia

On page 4 you saw how the people of the United States began growing a lot of cotton. The Australians did the same with wool. There were twenty-nine sheep in Australia in 1789. By 1850 there were 17 million. How did that help the British woollen industry, do you think?

CLASS ACTIVITY
Make a wall diagram to show the results of changes in the cotton industry.

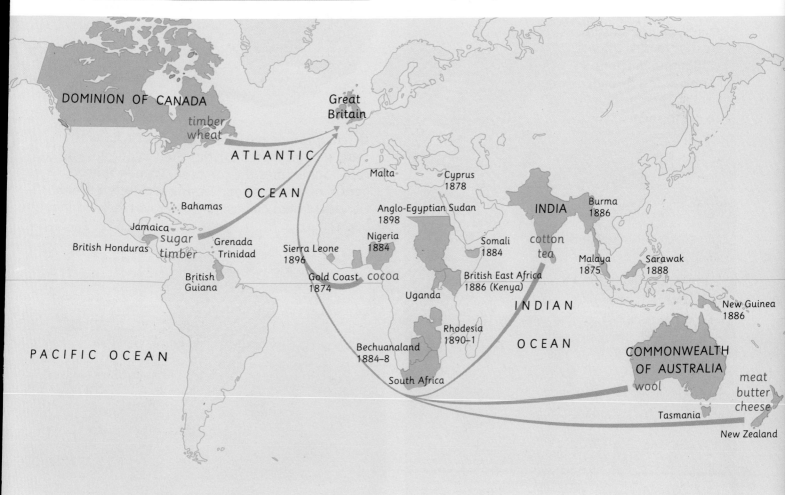

A Victorian map of the British Empire.

A factory boy of 1840

When people worked at home, they made their children help. The children had to get up early. They had to stay up late at night. Their parents often beat them. Also, the parents kept all the money the family earned.

When the new factories were built, children worked in them. This is the story of a factory boy of the 1830s.

Thomas Clarke lived in Leicester. When he was nine, he went to work in a woollen mill. There, he helped a young man called George Castles. Castles looked after a spinning machine. If any of the threads broke, Thomas had to mend them.

Thomas worked the same hours as Castles. He began at six in the morning. He finished at nine in the evening. He had two hours for meals. One Monday, Thomas began work at six as usual. He then worked until nine o'clock on Tuesday evening.

Often, Thomas fell asleep at work. Why was that, do you think? Castles then beat him with a rope. Sometimes the foreman, James Thorpe, beat him with a strap. Thorpe was often drunk. He would beat children just because he was in a bad temper.

One day Thomas was beaten so badly that he ran home. He showed his mother the bruises. She told him to go back to work. Why did she want him to do that, do you suppose? Thomas ran off. His mother caught him and beat him.

One day, Thomas went to sleep and fell into the machine. Luckily, he was not badly hurt. But he left the mill. He was then too old for his mother to stop him.

Thomas earned three shillings (15p) a week. His mother took it all. Sometimes she gave him a penny (less than $\frac{1}{2}$p) as pocket money. Thomas spent it on apples.

Thomas now spins ropes. His little brother, aged seven, helps him. Thomas keeps all his brother's wages. The other spinners sometimes beat their helpers. Thomas says he never does. Do you believe him?

CLASS ACTIVITY
Draw two time lines, each 24 hours. On one of them mark the hours that Thomas worked. On the other, mark the hours you spend working at school.

Handloom weavers in the 1840s

Here we will see what happened to the handloom weavers after the factories were built.

This is the kind of thing they were saying. Read it and look at the pictures:

When I was young I earned good wages. I had three suits of clothes, two pairs of shoes and several hats. I even had a gold watch. I never worked on Sundays. I used to take my wife and children to church. Monday was also a day of rest. I used to weave the other days of the week. But I was my own master. I could stop when I liked, and have a drink with my friends. We had our own room at the pub. It said 'Handloom weavers only' on the door.

Now I have to try to keep up with the power looms. It is impossible. I work fourteen hours a day, every day. I even work on Sundays. But my wages are only a quarter of what they were. My fine clothes are worn out. I am ashamed to go to church. My wife has to work in the factory. Without her wages we would starve.

How did the weaver spend his money when he was well off?

What did he do in his spare time?

How had the life of the handloom weaver changed?

What did the weaver blame for the change?

How does he feel about his wife's job, do you think?

A weaver and his family in the days before factories.

This is the kind of thing employers were saying:

In the old days I employed 500 weavers. They were scattered over three counties. Making sure they had their thread was difficult. Often, the cloth was uneven. The threads were tight in some places and loose in others. Often, the weavers were late finishing their work. That made my customers angry. Sometimes, the weavers even stole my thread.

It is much better now I have my power looms. They weave top quality cloth. I always finish my orders on time. No one ever steals my thread.

For what reasons is this man happy about the change to power looms?

Can you think of other people who might be happy about the change?

CLASS ACTIVITY
If you can find a small loom, bring it to your classroom. Let everyone see how it works.

Inside the factory where the weaver's wife was forced to work.

11

A girl coal-miner of 1840

Ann Ambler is fourteen. She and a boy called William Dyson work in a mine. The two children help a grown-up miner. He loosens the coal with his pick. He then shovels it into a little truck. This is called a **corve**.

When the corve is full, Ann drags it to the pit bottom.

Here, she hooks it on to the **clatch iron**. A woman at the top winds it to the surface.

Ann and William coming up the shaft. They are sitting on the clatch iron. The woman is working a 'turn wheel'. What will happen if she jerks the wheel and sets the children swinging? What will happen if she looks the other way and goes on winding for too long? What will happen if she loses her grip and lets go of the winding handle?

Ann now goes back to the coal face. The miner has already filled another corve.

She and William have to work very quickly. They are even called **hurriers**! The miner is very angry if they keep him waiting.

A hurrier dragging a corve full of coal from the coal face to the bottom of the mine shaft where it will be hauled to the surface.

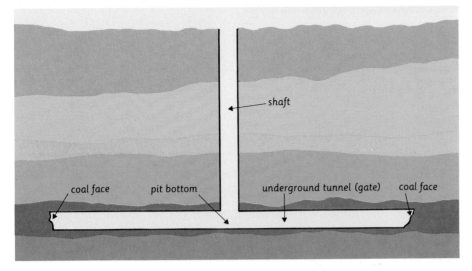

shaft

coal face   pit bottom   underground tunnel (gate)   coal face

Diagram of a coal mine. First a mine shaft would be dug down until it reached the coal. Then horizontal tunnels would be dug in the coal seam in all directions. As the coal was cut away, wooden pit-props were wedged between the floor and the roof of the tunnel to stop the ceiling from falling in.

The floor of the **gate** or underground tunnel is bumpy. In places, there is water. Wooden props hold up the roof, but sometimes heavy stones fall from it. A gas called methane seeps out of the coal. The miners know it as 'fire damp'. If there is enough of it, it will explode.

Ann starts work at seven in the morning. She eats her midday meal in the pit. She might finish at four in the afternoon. Often she works until six. Her wages are six shillings (30p) a week.

The mine where Ann works is small and old fashioned. Other mines are more modern. Ann's mine has only one steam engine, eighty years old. It pumps water out of the mine. Other mines have much better pumping engines. They also have winding engines which can lift much heavier loads than a woman with a turn wheel!

This is what William told some visitors to the mine:

Ann hurries the same weight and distances that I do. I have seen her thrashed many times, when she does not please the miners. They rap her in the face and knock her down. She does not like the work, she does not that. I have seen her cry many times.

People killed in mines, 1838	
Fell down shaft	66
Drawn over pulley	6
Drowned	15
Fall of stones	101
Explosions	84
Run over by waggons	12
Other causes	10
Total	294

An up-to-date mine. What danger was there here?

CLASS ACTIVITIES

Show the table of people killed in mines as a diagram. First decide what kind of diagram would be best.

Write and act a play in which a factory boy and a girl coal-miner talk about their work.

Town houses of the 1840s

You have already met Thomas Clarke, the factory boy from Leicester. We will now see what his home would have been like.

Poor people's houses were crammed together. Sometimes they were not only side by side in terraces. They were also back to back. Draw a plan of a row of back-to-back houses. How many walls in a house could have windows?

All but the main streets were narrow. With his arms outstretched, a man might be able to touch the houses on both sides. There could even be a house across one end of the street. If so, there was a tunnel passage through it.

Find the tunnel passage in this picture.

CLASS ACTIVITY
Talk about the way things tie up with each other. What were the results of having factories, but no buses and poor wages? Think of some other examples, from your own lives. Not all are bad!

A street with a partly blocked end was called a **court**. Draw a plan of a court.

Houses might be two, three or four storeys. There was just one room on each floor. Very likely, a whole family lived in each room.

A house might have a cellar. If so, it was home for yet another family. In 1839, 39,000 Liverpool people were living in 7860 cellars.

How many might you expect to find in one cellar?

Walls were only one brick in thickness. Damp came through them. Sometimes they were black with damp.

Roofs were of slates. Slates can make a very good roof. But in poor houses they did not overlap enough.

What happened then, do you think?

Houses were like this mainly because of the factories. Owners built their factories in towns, so that they could find workers. Then more and more factories were built and this meant more and more workers

London houses. What would it be like to live in one of them? There are some good descriptions in several novels by great Victorian writers, especially Charles Dickens. ('Hard Times').

were needed. People flocked to the towns. But in those days there were no buses.

How does that explain why the houses were crammed together?

Now look at the picture of the court on the previous page. Could people like that afford well built houses?

Look at pages 28-9. In what ways were rich people's houses better than those of the poor people?

15

A poor man's house

You are now going to see what it might have been like inside Thomas Clarke's house. To find out something like that we have to use sources. There are many kinds of sources. Two of the most useful are things people have written and things they have drawn.

Look carefully at the two pictures here. Both show rooms belonging to poor people. How are they alike? How are they different? Can you explain why they are different?

Then read the written sources describing poor houses in Bath and Willenhall.

In 1843 a man called R. H. Horne visited some poor houses in Willenhall. He wrote:

> I have entered very poor houses; no furniture but a broken board for a table and a plank laid across bricks for a seat; with the wife almost crying with hunger and in rags; yet the floor was perfectly clean. I have gone upstairs and seen a broken old bed with a sack for bedclothes and nothing else in the room. Yet the bed was clean; so was the floor; so were the stairs. They were not just clean they were really white.

16

A Bath clergyman visited three poor houses in the town. This is what he wrote:

> There was filth all over the place. The place was reeking with the smell of filth. The two beds were shining with body grease, but there was no covering on them.
>
> In the fire-grates the ashes had not been cleared away for a long time. The beds were rotten. Great bugs were crawling about them. The plaster was off the walls in many places. Broken windows had been stuffed with rags and sacks.
>
> A little boy was lying on the bed, naked except for a piece of cloth around his neck. He was ill and struggling for breath. He was sucking from a filthy feeding bottle which contained sour milk curds. I swept maggots from under the bed with a broom. I stirred up maggots from the bed itself with the handle of the broom.

Probably, you are a bit puzzled. Sources are like that. They tell us about the past. But they also leave us asking a lot of questions.

Make a list of all the things you have learnt from the sources. Use these facts to write your own description of poor people's houses.

CLASS ACTIVITIES

Several people should read their descriptions of poor houses to the class. Discuss them saying where you agree and disagree.

In groups decide what questions you would like to ask the sources. Which of these questions are the most important?

Dirt and disease

In early Victorian times, half the children in some big cities never grew up. They died before they were fifteen.

Could you think of some reasons for that from what you already know?

Now look at this picture on the right. The family lives in a cellar. One of the children is ill.

Why is this home unhealthy, do you think?

Look at the picture of the court on the left. The houses have no drains. But beside the boy is a deep gutter. It is called a **kennel**, which is another word for channel. What is the use of the kennel, do you think?

Behind the boy is the lavatory door. The lavatory is called the **privy**. It is just a pit with a wooden seat over it. Several families use the same privy. When the pit is full, men come and empty it.

The picture on the next page shows these men at work. What are they using?

They are only allowed to work at night. Why is that, do you think?

Some people pile all the filth from the privy in the street. Why is that unpleasant?

When the filth has rotted the people sell it to farmers. This is called dung. Why do the farmers want it?

There are no water taps in the houses.

There is just one outside tap for the whole street. Even worse, the water is turned on for less than an hour a day. When the water comes on, people crowd round the tap with buckets and pans. How do you think they behave?

In the end, none of them has much water. How do they make it go as far as possible, do you suppose?

Here, then, are lots of reasons why many people died of disease. There was another one as well.

No one knew about germs. They believed that bad smells caused disease. They thought the smells poisoned the air, just as the wrong things can poison food. This once led to a dreadful mistake.

From time to time a terrible disease called **cholera** came to Britain. It was most unpleasant and half the

people who caught it died. Everyone believed it was caused by bad smells. To get rid of the cholera, they thought they must get rid of the smells.

The government ordered that all the dung heaps in London should be thrown into the Thames. But the dung heaps were full of cholera germs. Also, much of London's drinking water came from the Thames. What do you suppose happened?

Father Thames introducing his offspring to the fair City of London. A 'Punch' cartoon, 1858.

19

The workhouse

The factories took jobs from the handloom weavers, but many other people were out of work as well.

Today, the unemployed have help, such as the dole. In Victorian times they had to go to the workhouse. They were then known as **paupers**.

The workhouse was somewhere to live. The paupers had food and clothing. There were, though, very strict rules.

Once inside the workhouse, a family was broken up. The mother might keep her baby, or a very young child. But the rest of the family went to other parts of the workhouse. There were separate yards and rooms for women, men, girls and boys.

Look at the picture of the workhouse and find the different yards.

Food was very dull. Mainly, the paupers lived on bread and gruel, a watery porridge. The only drink was water. No one had beer or wine. Smoking was forbidden.

Look at the people eating. This is a Christmas dinner! How is it different from your own Christmas dinner? Why are there no women?

A Manchester workhouse.

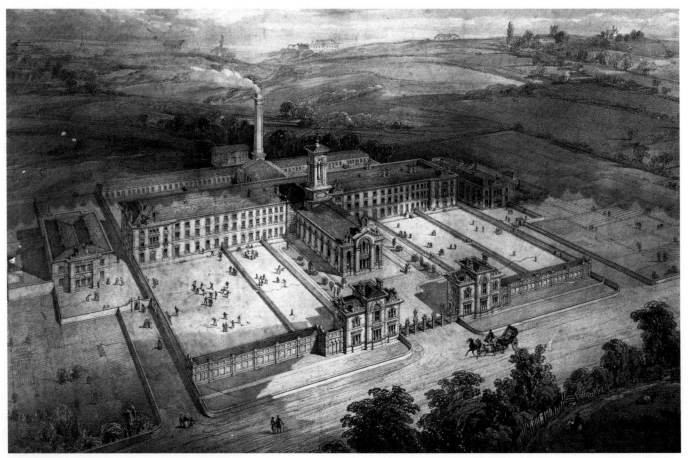

This Victorian photograph shows a meal in a workhouse.

The paupers had to do hard, dull work. The women washed clothes by hand. The picture below shows men at work.

What are they doing?

The idea behind the workhouse was to make lazy people find jobs.

Would anyone who lost his job try hard to find another? Which people found this system unfair, do you think?

What did people fear as they grew old?

Read the following story about the Andover workhouse. What does it tell you about the food there?

This is what a pauper in Andover workhouse said:

I worked at bone breaking. We looked out for the fresh bones, then we used to be after them like a pack of dogs. Sometimes I had one that was stale and stunk. I ate it because I was hungry. I have seen a man named Reeves eat horse flesh off the bones. I told him it was horse flesh. He did not care. It went down as sweet as a nut.

Clothing was an ugly uniform. Women were not allowed to look pretty. Men were not allowed to look smart.

Religion was very important. Some people thought that being poor was a punishment from God. The paupers went to chapel once every weekday and several times on Sundays.

Find the chapel in the picture of the workhouse opposite.

Chopping woo

Write

Schools for poor children in the 1840s

There are often big differences between present and past.

In the 1840s, children like Ann Ambler and Thomas Clarke left school when they were very young. Their parents sent them to work as soon as possible. There was no law to prevent this.

There were schools for poor children in all the big towns. But read this description of children in Wolverhampton:

> You will find boys who have never heard of London, nor of Willenhall (which is only three miles distant), who have never heard the name of the Queen, or who have believed it was Prince Albert. You will find poor girls who have never sung or danced; never read a book that made them laugh; never seen a violet or a primrose; whose only idea of a green field came from having been stung by a nettle.

Were the schools much good, do you think?

One kind of school was the Dame School. Parents paid the teacher a few pennies each week. They just wanted someone to look after the children while they went to work. The children learnt very little.

Look at the picture of the Dame School below. Read the following description:

> It was in an attic, up three flights of dark, broken stairs. There were forty children in a room ten feet by nine. On a perch sat a cock and two hens. Under a bed was a kennel with three terriers. The fowls were cackling; the dogs were barking; the children were making a noise. The teacher sat by the only window, keeping out most of the light.

Would it be easy to work in such a school?

Another kind of school was the Sunday School. These cost very little to run.

Sunday School teachers worked for nothing. Almost anyone could be a teacher. Some could not write. Some could not even read very well. Did Sunday School children learn very much, do you think?

A reading lesson in a Monitorial School.

A third kind of school was the Monitorial School. You will see why it had that name in a minute. Rich people gave the money for Monitorial Schools. But they did not give very much. The children wrote on slates.

Why was that cheaper than paper?

Instead of books there were reading sheets on the wall. How did that save money?

Look at the picture above of the reading lesson. How did the children use the sheets?

Worst of all, there was only enough money for one adult teacher.

The pictures of the Monitorial Schools on this page show how one teacher could teach a whole school.

Find the older children. They are the taller ones in the picture above and the ones standing up in the picture below. These were the **monitors**. Every morning they came to school early. The teacher gave them their lessons. Then the rest of the children arrived.

Each monitor took a group. He taught them what he had already learnt himself.

Find the teacher in the picture below. What is he doing?

The teacher also punished naughty children. One punishment was to put the child in a basket and hang it from the ceiling!

A writing lesson in a Monitorial School.

These pictures are of boys' schools. There were separate schools for girls but not many. What did people think about education for girls, do you suppose?

CLASS ACTIVITY

A Victorian child has been brought back to life. You show him round your school. Write and act a short play about it.

23

How poor people enjoyed themselves

You have read about poor people's houses. Many fathers did not want to spend their evenings at home. Why was that, do you think?

Often, the only place they could go was the public house. Look at this picture of one. What are the people doing?

Going to the pub cost money. How could that money have been better spent?

Some fathers did not go to the pubs very often. They were the ones who had other things to do.

For example, just outside Nottingham there were allotments. They were bigger than the allotments we have today. They were more interesting, too. As well as vegetables, the people grew fruit trees and flowers.

On each allotment was a summer-house. Here was a pleasant place for the family to go on a warm Sunday. What do you think they could do there?

Below is a famous Victorian painting by Frith. It is called Derby Day and shows another popular amusement. What is it?

Many handloom weavers kept racing pigeons. Read this story about two of them:

A weaver had a racing pigeon that won every race. Another weaver had a pigeon that always came second. This man tried to buy the champion bird. Its owner wanted a lot of money. To find it, the man sold his loom. That meant he could never work again. As soon as he had the pigeon he wrung its neck. 'Cook this for my supper,' he told his wife. When he had finished eating, he patted his stomach. 'Now my pigeon is the best,' he said.

Few children were given pocket money. They had to make their own amusements. The picture below shows some of them. What were they?

Children also played with buttons. First, they spread them on the ground. Then each player licked his thumb and picked up as many buttons as he could before it went dry.

What else could children do that did not cost money?

Children were sometimes naughty, especially boys. Gangs from rival schools fought each other.

The streets had gas lights. Every evening a lamplighter went round putting them on. Boys followed, putting them out.

People woke in the mornings to find their nice black railings had been painted bright yellow. A favourite trick was to tie a piece of string to a door knocker.

What happened then, do you think?

Boys might find a drunk, asleep on the ground. It was great fun to tickle his face with a feather on the end of a stick.

Think about these amusements. How are they like our own? How are they different?

CLASS ACTIVITY
Bring buttons to school and play the game with them. But dip your thumbs in water. Don't lick them!

A young lady's day

Tea in the conservatory. A painting by James Tissot. What are these people talking about, do you think? Do they seem happy? Would you like to spend an afternoon like this?

After the factories were built there were more rich people in Britain than ever before. It was not only the factory owners who became wealthy. So did many others.

In the next sections we will see how the rich lived. We will start with a day in the life of a rich man's daughter. Her name is Caroline. She is eighteen years old.

Caroline wakes up at eight o'clock. She rings a bell. A maid comes to the bedroom.

She draws back the curtains and lights the fire. She then fetches Caroline's breakfast.

After breakfast, Caroline has her bath. She uses a hip bath, in front of the fire. The maid has to fill it with warm water. She carries the water up two flights of stairs from the kitchen.

When she has dressed, Caroline joins her mother and sister in the drawing-room. They spend the morning doing fine embroidery. All are very good at it.

After a light lunch, the mother and the two girls go out in their carriage. They call on friends. If a lady does not want visitors the servant says she is 'not at home'. Caroline's mother then leaves her card. She bends the corner to show that she called in person. If a friend is 'at home', they join her for tea.

There are many rules about good manners. Caroline can hardly remember them all.

When she returns home, Caroline goes to her room. The maid brings her warm water for washing. Caroline changes and goes down to dinner.

Her father has now returned from his office. He sits at the head of the table.

The dinner is a big meal of three courses.

The family spends the rest of the evening in the drawing-room. The mother plays the piano. The girls sing. The father may read to them. At eleven o'clock, the servants are called in for prayers. Everyone then goes to bed.

Do you think Caroline leads a useful life?

How would many women feel today, if they had to lead lives like Caroline's?

How is Caroline's life different from Ann Ambler's (see pages 12-13)?

A tale of good manners:

Some country women were invited to have tea with Queen Victoria. One of the women dropped a piece of cake on the carpet. She blushed red.

A lady-in-waiting was amused and smiled. The Queen saw the smile. She dropped some cake herself, on purpose. She then made the lady-in-waiting pick up both pieces.

Serving at the dinner table. Who has laid the table? Who will be doing the washing up, do you think? What things will need great care? If dinner begins at eight, when will the washing up be finished, do you suppose?

The homes of the rich

Look at this picture of a rich family's house. How is it different from a modern house? Look at the bedroom below. How is it different from the bedrooms in your home? Now look at the photo of the ornaments in the Class Activity opposite. Would you want to dust all that? Who did dust it, do you think?

Rich Victorians liked to be comfortable. A French writer, Henri Taine, once visited England. The luxury in the rich houses amazed him. In the box below is a list of the things he found in his bedroom, just for washing. Imagine making a list of everything in the house!

A bedroom in a Victorian house.

Things for washing in one bedroom:

Looking-glass
Large jug
Medium-sized jug
Small jug
Two porcelain basins, for
    washing in
Dish for toothbrushes
Two soap-dishes
Water bottle and tumbler
Napkins underneath
    everything so far
Zinc bath
Towel-horse
Four towels of different
    kinds

You have already seen that the Victorians tried to make Britain modern. How did they do that?

In their homes, it was very different. The lavatory or water closet (WC) was about the only modern thing in most rich homes! Even so, people would not use it at night. They had chamber pots in their bedrooms.

A water closet.

28

The Victorians heated their homes with coal or log fires. These fires made a lot of work and a lot of dust. Would one of them warm a whole room, do you think?

The Victorians knew about central heating. They put it in some of their public buildings. But they would not have it at home. They said it was unhealthy, even though they caught colds the whole time!

Now think of all the electrical gadgets you have in your home. The Victorians could not have electricity in their homes, but they could have gas and there were gas stoves. Even so, few homes had one. There were coal-fired ranges instead.

All this seems strange to us, but there was a reason. Many girls and women became servants. It was they who dusted the rooms, emptied the chamber pots, carried the coal and did the cooking.

Spending money on things like gas stoves just made life easier for the servants. Rich Victorians saw no point in that!

Look at pages 14–19. In what ways were the homes of rich people better than those of poor people?

CLASS ACTIVITY

Everyone counts the pictures and ornaments in the living room at home. Work out the average for the class.

Now count the pictures and ornaments in the picture here. Just be as accurate as you can! Now compare that number with your own average.

Ladies' fashions

The Victorians had machines for making cloth. But, for a long time, they did not have machines to turn the cloth into clothes.

Women did the sewing by hand. They worked at home or in small workshops. They had very poor wages.

Now look at the pictures on these two pages. Each one is telling us different things. Read the poem. Which of the pictures does it match?

Look at pages 14–18 and 26. How were rich people's clothes different from those worn by poor people? Were they alike in any way?

VETO.

"SHALL WE—A—SIT DOWN?"   "I SHOULD LIKE TO; BUT MY DRESSMAKER SAYS I MUSTN'T!"

A cartoon from the magazine, Punch.

With fingers weary and worn,
With eyelids heavy and red,
A woman sat, in unwomanly rags,
Plying her needle and thread.
Stitch – stitch – stitch,
In poverty hunger and dirt,
And still with a voice of a dolorous pitch
She sang the Song of the Shirt.

Work – work – work,
My labour never flags;
And what are its wages? A bed of straw,
A crust of bread – and rags,
That shatter'd roof – and this naked floor –
A table – a broken chair –
And a wall so blank, my shadow I thank,
For sometimes falling there.

from '*The Song of the Shirt*' by Thomas Hood

A fashion plate advertising day dresses.

'Too Early' – a painting by James Tissot.

A cartoon of a dressmaker's workshop.

Railways

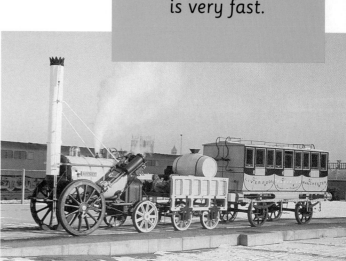

A great event happened in Lancashire in 1830. A railway was opened between Liverpool and Manchester. Find the two towns on a map. How far apart are they, roughly?

There had been railways in Britain for hundreds of years. But most of them belonged to coal mines. They carried the coal to the nearest river or canal. Also, trains on the early railways were drawn by horses.

The Liverpool to Manchester line was different. It was a public railway. That meant anyone could travel on it. Instead of horses there were steam locomotives.

One of them was the *Rocket*. It could travel at thirty miles an hour! It was made by the same man who built the railway – George Stephenson.

The Liverpool to Manchester line was a success. Soon, other people began to copy it. Robert Stephenson, George Stephenson's son, built the London to Birmingham line. It opened in 1838.

Look carefully at this Victorian painting by Frith. It is called 'The Railway Station'. What are some of the things that are happening? Find two detectives arresting a man. How is this station like a modern one? How is it different?

Isambard Kingdom Brunel built the Great Western Railway between London and Bristol. It was finished in 1841. Even so, Britain only had 500 miles of public railway by that time. However, between 1844 and 1850, 5000 miles of railway were built. In 1851 people from all parts of the country travelled by railway to the Great Exhibition in London.

A quarter of a million men had been hard at work making the railways. Brickworks, engineering and iron works and coal mines worked hard to supply the materials needed. When it was over, there were railways joining all of Britain's large towns. Nothing so big and important had ever happened so quickly before.

All the embankments, cuttings and tunnels were made by hand by men called 'navvies'. They only had picks, shovels and wheelbarrows.

Digging a cutting. Wheelbarrows are filled with earth and then horses pull them up the planks with ropes. The men guide the wheelbarrows.

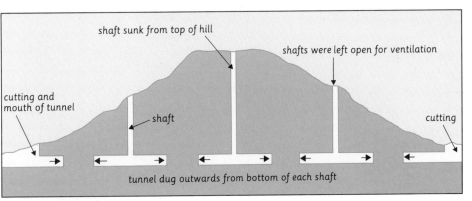

This diagram shows you how they made tunnels. Why didn't they just dig from either end, do you think?

There were as many dangers in digging railway tunnels as there were in coal mines (see pages 12–13). What were those dangers?

When digging a tunnel, three navvies in every hundred might die. That was the same as the number of British soldiers killed at the Battle of Waterloo.

CLASS ACTIVITY
Find a railway on a large scale map.
Measure out ten miles.

How much of the distance is
a) cutting; b) embankment; c) tunnel?

This will show you how much work is needed to make a railway.

The world of work in the 1890s

Queen Victoria died in 1901. She had come to the throne in 1837. Britain had changed a great deal during her long reign. But not all the changes were very rapid.

In 1837, cotton was a young industry. By the time Victoria died, the factories still worked in much the same way. But there were more of them, and they were bigger.

Nearly three quarters of the world's cotton cloth was made in Lancashire. Problems were already appearing, though. Countries that grew cotton were building their own factories. Two such countries were the United States and India.

Also, in about 1890, the French began making rayon. It was the first of the man-made fibres. They called it 'artificial silk'. How did these changes affect the cotton factories in Britain, do you think?

In the mines, there were still no machines for cutting coal. Men still did that with picks and shovels. But there were few little mines, like Ann Ambler's.

Most mines were large. They used pit ponies to transport the coal underground. They used steam engines to wind it to the surface. These things were not new. It was just that all pits had them, instead of a few.

Also, there were a million miners in 1900. In 1840, there had been 200,000.

Queen Victoria's funeral.

Look at this picture. Compare it with the winding gear shown on page 12. Which mine will produce more coal? Why?

Pit head winding gear of 1900.

At the end of Victoria's reign, Britain produced a quarter of the world's coal. But a newer and better fuel had been discovered. This was oil.

How do we use coal today? How do we use oil? (Remember what we make from it!)

As you know, the cotton factories had steam engines to drive their machines. Steam engines were too big for workshops.

Then, in 1859, a Frenchman called Lenoir invented a gas engine. It was small and it was easy to start and stop. By then, every town had a gas works. Soon, many workshops had Lenoir engines.

They were very useful in the clothing trades. They drove the looms that knitted stockings, and the sewing machines that made clothes and shoes.

The Lenoir engine was an **internal combustion engine**. Very likely, your family has an engine of this kind. What does it drive?

A jet workshop in Whitby. Jet is a hard black mineral that can be polished like a gemstone and used to make jewellery.

Look at this picture of a workshop. Find the wheels that drive the machines. What power drives machines today?

CLASS ACTIVITY
This is for people interested in science and technology. Find out how an internal combustion engine works. Then prepare some wall charts to explain it to the rest of the class.

The importance of cheap steel

The Forth Bridge soon after its opening in 1890.

In early Victorian times there was plenty of cheap **iron**. It was used for machines and railways. But there was no cheap **steel**.

Steel is a special kind of iron. It is much stronger. A small piece of steel will do the same job as a large piece of iron.

For example, an iron ship needs thick sides. That makes it heavy. A steel ship can have thinner sides. That makes it much lighter.

Which ship can carry more cargo?

For a long time steel was very expensive. It was only used in things like knives and tools. Then, in 1856, a man called Henry Bessemer found a way of making cheap steel. In 1866 William Siemens found an even better method.

People could now have all the steel they wanted. The illustrations show you some of the things they made from it.

Think of some of the results of making these things.

Think of some other things that are made from steel.

Try to imagine life without steel. That will show you how important Bessemer and Siemens were!

36

Mauretania at Landing Stage, Liverpool

The Mauretania. This ship was built only six years after Queen Victoria died.

The advertisement below is for British bicycles on sale in Paris, in about 1900.

SINGER CYCLES

Singer & Co. PARIS 45, AVᵉ de la Gᵈᵉ ARMEE. COVENTRY, ENGLAND.

THE DANGERFIELD PRINTING Cᵒ LONDON.

Three Benz motor cars of the 1890s. In 1894 a German called Daimler invented a new engine. It was an internal combustion engine, like Lenoir's, but it burnt petrol vapour, not gas. Soon afterwards another German called Benz used the petrol engine to power the first cars ever built.

CLASS ACTIVITIES

1. Draw pictures of things made from steel. Mount the pictures on a wall chart.
2. Use a word processor to write a leaflet about the importance of steel.

Heavy guns on a warship.

Daily life in the 1890s

During Victoria's reign the population of Great Britain doubled to reach 42 million. This was mainly because people were living longer and leading more pleasant lives. There were many reasons for this.

Scientists made new discoveries. In 1847, a doctor called James Simpson found he could put people to sleep for operations. He used **chloroform**. How did that help save lives?

Many people still died though. Their wounds went septic. Then, in the 1860s, the French scientist Louis Pasteur discovered **microbes**. Some microbes caused disease and make wounds go septic. We call this kind 'germs'.

Another English doctor, Lord Lister, heard of Pasteur's work. He began using **antiseptics** to kill germs during operations.

A photograph of Victorian houses in Nightingale Lane, Hornsey, London, taken in about 1890.

Something very different also happened. People like the Earl of Shaftesbury persuaded Parliament to pass laws protecting children.

One law said that children must not work in factories. Another said they must not work in mines. Later, a third law said that children must go to school.

How did the third law make sure people obeyed the other two?

There were big improvements in the cities. They now had sewers and also new waterworks. Most houses had indoor taps. Also, the water was on all the time. Why were these changes important?

Many slums were cleared away. Instead of courts and alleys there were wide, new streets.

Look at the photographs of late-Victorian streets on this page. Compare them with the pictures on pages 14–15 and 18–19.

Where would you rather live? Why?

A late-Victorian street as it appears today.

By the end of Victoria's reign every town had a park. People could walk in the park and enjoy themselves. Often there was a bandstand where open-air concerts took place at the weekend.

The railways brought many changes. For one thing, people were able to go to the seaside. New seaside towns sprang up. One of them was Bournemouth. After the railways came it grew into a big town.

What seaside towns have you visited? How did you travel to them?

On the beach at Southsea in the 1890s.

Once, people had to live near to their work.

Why was that?

Now look at this picture. These vehicles appeared in many cities. Where could people live now?

London also had another kind of transport. It ran beneath the streets.

What was it?

An electric tram in Camborne, Cornwall. London first had horse-drawn buses. In the 1860s it had horse-drawn trams. They ran more easily because they were on rails. After 1891 there were electric trams. The first motor-buses appeared in 1898. In the end, they put the trams out of business.

Rich people did not improve their houses much. This picture shows one of the few changes they made, but a lady still needed a servant to help her have her bath!

There are sometimes
big differences between the past
and the present.

Religion

A visitor to Wolverhampton once asked a miner what he knew about Jesus. 'Who's that?' asked the man. 'Does he work down the pit?'

This kind of thing shocked many Victorians. They thought it was dreadful not to know about God and Jesus. Rich people gave money to build schools for the poor. They wanted children to learn about religion. This was the most important school subject.

People often went to church. They were also very religious in their own homes.

Look at the painting below. What book is the father reading, do you think?

Look at the cartoon of the little girl with her mother. What is she doing?

THE FORCE OF EXAMPLE.

"Now, Jessie, say your Prayers like a good little Girl!"
"Mamma, dear! why mayn't I kneel down, and hold my tongue, as Papa does?"

This is what an old man remembered about Sundays. He had two brothers:

Victorian children going to church to attend Sunday School.

We came down to breakfast at 8 o'clock. We had already oiled our hair and polished our shoes.

At quarter past nine we went to Sunday School. That lasted until 11 o'clock. We then went straight to church. Our parents joined us. The service seemed to last for ever. The worst part was the sermon.

After church we went for a walk in the park. During the week we wore comfortable caps. On Sundays we wore 'Mr Palmer's boys' bowlers, price one shilling'.

Our parents wore their best clothes and made rude remarks about what the neighbours were wearing.

At lunch, Father would ask us what the vicar had said in his sermon. We were in trouble if we did not know. When lunch was over, it was back to Sunday School. That ended at half-past four. We might then escape the grown-ups for a while. We could read 'Sunday at Home'. But we suffered a fate worse than death if Father caught us with a comic.

The family went to church again at six. We then came home to supper, evening prayers and bed.

We had our revenge one day. The vicar went into the church and left the key in the lock. Can you guess what we did? He had to ring the bell until someone let him out.

CLASS ACTIVITY
In Victorian times, nearly everyone went to a place of worship on Sunday.
Hold a secret ballot to find out how many in your class do so, and also what places of worship they attend.

How many times did the boys go to Sunday School?

How many times did they go to church?

What else did the boys dislike about Sunday?

How is your Sunday different?

Is it the same in any way?

Weymouth House School, Bath, in the 1890s

The next six pages tell you about a school in the 1890s. When you have read them you, too, should write the history of a school. There are some notes at the end of the last page to help you.

Weymouth House School was on two floors. Part of the ground floor was a covered playground. Children were glad of it in bad weather. They were never allowed in the classrooms during playtime.

Girls' school room, Weymouth House.

An old pupil called Frank Giddings tells us about it:

Two coal-fired boilers served food to the children at a half-penny a time. Monday, a large basin of boiled rice; Wednesday, Irish Stew with plenty of meat; Friday, currant roly-poly.

The first floor was divided into two. One half was for boys and one half for girls. This picture shows the girls' school.

In the early days, the head teacher needed to see all the pupils. Look back to pages 22 and 23 if you have forgotten why.

Later, teachers wanted to separate the classes. All they could do at Weymouth House was hang curtains between them.

Find the poles that supported the curtains. They are about two metres from the ground.

One corner is walled off. This was the girls' 'bonnet room'. The boys hung their caps and their coats in the classroom.

Why was that unpleasant in wet weather?

How is the classroom furniture different from your own? Which is better, do you think? The back desks in each group are on platforms. Why was that do you think?

Frank Giddings tells us about the heating at Weymouth House:

> There was just one stove. The headmaster used to hug the fire, while the boys shivered.

Head teachers used to keep diaries, called log books. Here are two entries from the headmistress's:

> 24 April 1893. Children sleepy and careless owing to the pressing heat. Temperature at 85° with all doors and windows open.

> 9 February 1895. The temperature of the room at 9.30 a.m. was 32°. With the help of the gas lights we got it up higher as the morning went on. The lessons were omitted and drill, marching and singing were taken instead.

Look this Victorian photograph of girls in a classroom in another school. Now imagine Weymouth House School full of children.

Two Victorian schools. The larger one above is at Camberwell in south-east London. The smaller one is at Poole in Dorset.

CLASS ACTIVITY
Rule a piece of paper down the middle. On the left put down all you can find about Weymouth House School. On the right put the same kind of information about your own school. Are the two schools alike in any way?

Teachers at Weymouth House School

There were differences between different times in the past.

At the beginning of Victoria's reign most teachers were **monitors** (see pages 22-3). If you were a monitor, you were just one of the older children in the school.

When you were about eleven, you left to find other work. But from about 1850, schools began to have **pupil teachers**.

You became a pupil teacher at twelve. It was part of the head's job to train you to become a proper teacher. He did this after school. In return you taught in the school during the day.

When you were eighteen or nineteen you became an **assistant teacher**. Later, if you passed a difficult examination, you might become a **head teacher**. Who is your head teacher? Name some of the assistant teachers.

The photograph below shows a class with an assistant teacher and a pupil teacher. Can you tell the two teachers apart?

By the 1890s most schools had one or two assistant teachers and several pupil teachers.

The younger pupil teachers worked with the head. But the older ones and the assistant teachers took classes on their own. Some were lucky enough to have their own classrooms. How did they separate the classes at Weymouth House School?

Frank Giddings tells us about his headmaster at Weymouth House:

> Mr. Swanson was very strict. He treated us as if we were soldiers. He made us march and salute. Every morning he inspected us to see if we had washed our faces and cleaned our shoes. He caned any boy who misbehaved. But if he confiscated any sweets, he gave them back at the end of the day. When he met us in the town, he always stopped for a chat. We were rather afraid of him, but we liked him.

How did Mr. Swanson keep discipline in his school?

Are any of these methods used today?

Why did Mr. Swanson's pupils like him?

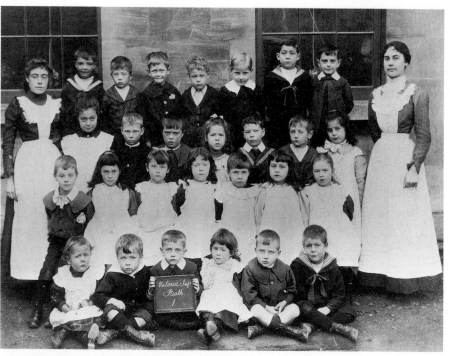

An infants' class.

Here are some complaints about a pupil teacher called Arthur Clements:

1. Absenting himself without permission from 10 May to 16 May.
2. Sending scholars to buy whisky during school hours.
3. Drinking whisky in the presence of his class.
4. Breaking open with a poker, a cupboard in the school from which a collection box was lost (contents included).

What happened to Arthur Clements, do you suppose?

Look at the photographs of two pages from a school log book on the right. They were written by the head teacher of an infants' school. She is complaining about a pupil teacher.

Most pupil teachers behaved well. We only hear about the ones who behaved badly. Why is that, do you think?

Children at Weymouth House School

There are important differences between past and present.

A visiting school inspector asking one of the young pupils a question.

Today, most schools group children by age.

How old are the children in your class?

When will you go up a class?

In Victorian times, schools grouped children by the work they could do. They called the groups **standards**.

All children went into Standard 1 when they left the infants' school. They hoped to go up a standard each year. But once a year an inspector came to the school. He set an examination.

The children who passed went up a standard. Those who failed stayed down for another whole year. Some children never left Standard 1!

Look at the table in the next column. It shows you the number of boys in every standard at Weymouth House School in 1893. It also shows their ages.

Some figures are underlined. They are the

boys in the right standard for their ages. They had passed their examination every single year.

Age	Numbers in each standard						
	1	2	3	4	5	6	7
7	36						
8	16	11					
9	19	9	5	1			
10	8	8	11	8			
11	3	8	8	11	4		
12	3	4	5	15	8		
13		1	3	7	3		
14			1		1	1	

How many standards were there?

What were the ages of the youngest and oldest boys in the school?

46

Add up the numbers in each standard. Which is the biggest?

What was the age of the youngest boys in Standard 1? What was the age of the oldest? How many times had the oldest boys failed the Standard 1 examination?

How many boys were in the right standard for their ages? How many were above it? How many were below?

Children could leave school the day they were thirteen. They could leave younger than that, if they had passed Standard 4.

How many boys were staying in the school longer than they needed?

A man called William Eyles said this about his school days in Bath:

I don't remember much about my school. I wasn't often there. Sometimes I wandered off before school. Sometimes I jumped the fence at play-time. The teacher used to cane me. My father would give me the strap. But that didn't stop me.

I didn't like school. I didn't like having three cuts on either hand with the cane... I didn't like the way the young assistant teachers used to pick on me. The pupil teachers were just as bad.

I never got further than Standard 2. I knew nothing when I left school. But I learned to read, write and reckon as soon as I left. I became an errand boy, you see. I had to collect orders from the customers.

Which standard did William reach? Why didn't he do any better? Was it because he was stupid?

Do you think there were many children like William?

DISCOVERING VICTORIAN SCHOOLS

Discover what you can about all the old schools in your area. You can then decide whether to write about one of them, several of them, or all of them.

1. Start with your own family. Can your grandparents remember anything their parents and grandparents told them? Have you any old letters, diaries, photographs or books?

2. Are there any schools in your area that look like the ones on pages 42 and 43? You may even attend one! See if the building has a date on it. If you can visit the building, draw a rough plan of it. Try to decide which bits are old and which are newer. The smaller school shown in the photograph on page 43 has had a bit added, which you should be able to spot. The biggest room would have been the 'school room', where the head taught several classes. Now it might be the hall, or it might have been divided.

3. Ask the local library for histories of the area, or any other books which give information about schools. Have they any old guidebooks, directories or maps?

4. Visit your local museum and see if it has anything on schools.

5. If you attend an old school, ask your head if there are any records, especially log books. Log books were diaries that head teachers kept. If the log books are not in the school, ask your teacher to find them and make photocopies of some of the pages. The log books may be in the county or town archives, or in the education offices. Log books can tell us all sorts of things about schools, for example: buildings, children, parents, teachers, lessons, discipline, attendance.

6. Keep all the information you can find in a file or store it on your computer. Then make a display, or use your word processor to write an account.

Index